Confederate States Military Prison at Salisbury, NC

by
Dr. A. W. Mangum

Compiled by Donna Peeler Poteat

REPRINTED BY

Wake Forest, NC
www.scuppernongpress.com

Confederate States Military Prison at Salisbury, NC

By Dr. A. W. Mangum
Compiled by Donna Peeler Poteat

©2019 The Scuppernong Press

First Printing

The Scuppernong Press
PO Box 1724
Wake Forest, NC 27588
www.scuppernongpress.com

Cover and book design by Frank B. Powell, III

All rights reserved

Printed in the United States of America

No part of this book may be reproduced or transmitted in any form or by any means, electronic or mechanical, including photocopying, recording, or by any information and storage and retrieval system, without written permission from the editor and/or publisher.

International Standard Book Number
ISBN 978-1-942806-25-7

Library of Congress Control Number: 2019955708

─◦ Contents ◦─

Introduction .... *iii*

Part I — 10,000 Prisoners at a Time 1
The Factory Becomes a Prison 3
A Prisoner's Prophecy 6
About Suspending the *Habeas Corpus* Writ 9
The Prison's Better Days 11
Methods of Escape 13
Inquiries About Political Prisoners 14
Prison Horrors 17
Yankee Ingenuity in Providing Shelter 19

Part II — A Revolt of the Prisoners 21
An Accident 22
Climbing Oaks for Acorns 25
A Surgeon Gave His Life for the Prisoners 27
Preaching to the Prisoners 29
Escapes From the Prison 32
An Exchange of Prisoners 35
Escaped Prisoners Blamed Edwin M. Stanton 36

T. W. Hall Letter 41

Adolphus W. Mangum 51

THE CONFEDERATE MILITARY PRISON AT SALISBURY, NORTH CAROLINA, WHERE MANY UNION PRISONERS ARE CONFINED.—[DRAWN BY SERGEANT WILL, 20TH MASSACHUSETTS VOLUNTEERS.]

Introduction

While going through local 19th century newspapers online, I came across this two-installment article written in 1893 by Rev. Dr. A. W. Mangum about his time spent at the Salisbury Confederate Prison. The article carried so much information, it was surprising it had never been reprinted.

These articles led me to search in the *Official Records* for more information about the Salisbury Prison. There I found an extensive letter on the horrific conditions of the Salisbury Prison written February 17, 1865, by T. W. Hall, Assistant Adjutant and Inspector General. This letter is included at the end of this book. If you would like to real the entire letter with all of its enclosures, you can find it in the "War of the Rebellion: Serial 121" beginning on page 249.

— Donna Peeler Poteat
Salisbury, NC

Dr. A. W. Mangum

The Charlotte Observer
Sunday, May 28, 1893,
Salisbury Prison
10,000 Prisoners at a Time
Dr. Mangum's Graphic Description

Of the Necessary and Unavoidable Horrors of a Confederate States Prison — The Prisoners' Food and Shelter Was as Good as Our Own Soldiers in the Field Had — A Striking Contrast Between the Condition of the Prisoners in the Earlier Days of the Confederacy and at the Last — The Mysterious Murders by the "Muggers" — How a Ventriloquist Effected the Escape of a Detail — A Tunnel Discovered — Burrows in the Earth for Purposes of Shelter.

The *Observer* today prints the first of two installments of the history of the "Confederate States Military Prison," at Salisbury, from the pen of Dr. A. W. Mangum, who was professor of mental and moral philosophy at the University of North Carolina at the time of his death in May, 1890. Dr. Mangum was living in Salisbury during part of the time the prison was filled with Federal captives and Confederate Convicts, and therefore was thoroughly conversant with the conduct of the institution. He was often during that period found as a follower of the meek and lowly Galilean, giving a cup of cold water to the lonely, home-sick, wretched prisoners. His history of the prison is an invaluable contribution to the history of the War Between the States, and even those of our Northern brethren, who may be prone to condemn the cruelty of Confederate prisons, must admit that the article is fair, withholding none of the horrors of the prison, but showing that the prison officers did the best they could without any means or money.

The second installment will be published in next Sunday's *Observer* and will contain, among other things, the terrible story of the last days of the prison, of an attempt of the prisoners to escape in a body, of the joyful occasion of an exchange and of the final destruction of the prison by Stoneman.

****

On the 19th of February 1839, a few of the enterprising, public-spirited and wealthy citizens of Salisbury, N.C., and the vicinity resolved to establish in the town a large steam cotton factory. On the 4th of April following the company was organized and applied themselves with energy to their commendable enterprise. The establishment was located in the beautiful oak grove that bordered the town on the south. The company secured about sixteen acres of the surrounding grounds. It was not long before the grove was vocal with the lively buzz and rattle of the machinery and the cheerful song and laughter of the busy factory boys and girls. Those were the halcyon days of peace and the daily picture in the grove was as full of beauty and pleasantness as it was of labor and life.

A few years passed in that way, when the factory was closed, the company dissolved and finally the property passed into the hands of the trustees of Davidson College.

Again, after a season, the solitude and stillness of the place were cheerily disturbed by a school of happy, hopeful boys. Their young forms glided over the shaded lawn in the joy of boyhood's sport, and their gay laughter and shouting rang richly through the dark, green boughs. And those, too, were the halcyon days of peace, and the daily picture in the grove was as full of beauty and innocence as it was of promise and life.

But soon a melancholy change came over our peaceful, prosperous land. A dark, dark shadow fell on its fair bosom, which carried shuddering to its heart — and made the hearts of the millions that rested on its bosom to shudder. It was the shadow of the black wing of war, "sprinkled red with human gore." It darkened our homes, while it darkened all others. It chilled our hearts as it chilled millions of others. It hushed our songs, it made our lips to quiver, and bent our knees for such prayers as our hearts had never dreamed before. It shed its baneful spell on all our scenes of beauty, on all our treasures of hope and love. It was the spirit of blighting, of desolation, of agony, of death. Where is the heart, the home, the plan, the prospect, that it did not change? And who can tell the measure of the woe of its changes?

The Factory Becomes a Prison

By a deed bearing date the 2nd of November, 1861, the old factory lot and buildings were conveyed to the Confederate States, and were fitted up and used during the four years of the war as a prison for Confederates under sentence of court martial, and those arrested for alleged disloyalty, for deserters from the Federal army and for prisoners of war.

A company composed of the students of Trinity College, styling themselves the "Trinity Guards," and commanded by Rev. Dr. B. Craven, their president, arrived and went into quarters at the garrison, with the duty of acting as guard to the prison. The first lot of prisoners, numbering one hundred and twenty, was brought in by the train on the 9th of December, 1861. Their arrival caused considerable excitement in the town, very few of the citizens having seen a "live Yankee soldier" up to that time. Their imprisonment was probably attended by as few discomforts and privations as regular prisoners of war were ever required to bear. They were quartered in the large, brick building (which was 100 x 40 feet, with three stories above the basement). Some of them were allowed the parole of the town. They strolled carelessly and cheerfully through the grounds, laughed and chatted in their warm quarters, tattooed their arms with the "Stars and Stripes," whittled on fancy toys and Yankee notions, etc., etc. When the commandant went in amongst them his language, his tone, the attention and respect, the quiet discipline and genial humor reminded one rather more of a pleasant scene in a college chapel than of rigid confinement in a prison.

On the 26th of December, when all the community was enjoying the annual festival commemorating the birth of the Prince of Peace, who came upon earth "to loose the prisoners," another train of cars came in, with the guards upon the platforms, bringing one hundred and seventy-six more prisoners.

Dr. Craven and his boys remained but a few weeks, and Col. George C. Gibbs was assigned to the command of the prison. The guard was composed of several companies raised for the purpose. A number of the citizens of Salisbury joined the guard.

On the 7th of February there was another arrival of eighty prisoners. These different installments came from various points — some being captured in Virginia, some on the coast of North Carolina and some by the Army of the west in Kentucky. By the middle of March, 1862, their number aggregated nearly 1,500. In December previous, Dr. J. W. Hall, of Salisbury, was appointed surgeon of the post. His report for the month of March, 1862, is the best commentary on the treatment of the prisoners, the fidelity of the officers, the care and attention of the surgeons and the management of the hospitals. That report states there were 1,427 prisoners, of which 251 had been under treatment, and only one had died. Compared with the daily reports of many of our regiments in the field, this showed that the suffering and loss among the latter was at least twenty times greater. The quarterly report, which was dated about the 21st of April, embracing from the 26th of December to that date, stated that of the guard there had been 509 cases of sickness, and but three deaths — of the prisoners, 403 cases, and only three deaths. Proportionally, there had been more sickness among the guard. Let it be remembered that this was the treatment the Confederate government gave its prisoners, while its resources were yet abundant, and it possessed the power to be humane in practice as it was in principle.

During this year even the ladies visited the grounds inside the stockade. Dress parade by the troops of the garrison was held near the southeast corner and witnessed by many of the prisoners. I remember attending the parade one pleasant summer evening in company with a number of ladies. When it was finished the officers among the prisoners came out and presented truly a beautiful scene in their recreation. A number of the younger and less dignified ran like schoolboys to the play ground, and were soon joining in high glee in a game of ball. Others, arm in arm, promenaded and conversed, while several sat down side by side with the prison officials and witnessed the sport and indulged in free and gentlemanly intercourse. I remarked particularly the tall form of Col. Corcoran (captured at Manassas) who, as he walked with measured step, and sad countenance, told plainly how deeply his pride was wounded – how severely his spirit was chafed.

A Prisoner's Prophecy

I remember a conversation with Major Vogdes, in which he prophesied the exhaustion of the supplies of the Confederacy and marked with his cane upon the ground how the State might, and probably would be, invaded on the lines of the railroads, and all opposition overcome. The position of Sherman's army at the finale of the struggle was similar to the diagram which he drew.

When Col. Gibbs completed his regiment, and left for service in the field, Col. A. C. Godwin took command of the prison. Like Col. Gibbs, he was a gentleman and a soldier. His management of the prison may be inferred from the fact that, while he was occupying a similar post in Richmond, he showed himself so generous to some Federal officers that, when he was captured on the Rappahannock and sent to the Northern prisons, he was sought out and signally favored in grateful return by either the individuals he had kindly served in their captivity, or by their relatives and friends.

It was during his command that a lofty flag pole was erected near the main entrance in front of headquarters, and a number of citizens, including ladies, went down to witness the raising of the Confederate flag.

When the cartel for exchange of prisoners was agreed upon by the commissioners of the two governments, all the prisoners of war were exchanged. This left only Confederate convicts, Yankee deserters and political prisoners.

The following official documents, together with a list of the civilian prisoners, copied from a paper kindly furnished by Gov. Swain, is published with the conviction that while they indicate the government in the premises, they will be of interest to many in the future:

Richmond, Va., }
February 27th, 1863. }

To the House of Representatives:

I herewith transmit a communication from the Secretary of War, covering a list of the civilian prisoners now in custody at the military prison at Salisbury, N.C., in further response to your resolution of the 5th inst., and invite attention to the recommendation in regard to a class of officers to be charged with the special duty of inquiring into the cases of prisoners arrested by military authority. I think such officers would be useful, they being selected for special qualifications and invested with special powers.

Jefferson Davis.

Confederate States of America, }
   War Department, }
Richmond, Va., February 27th, 1863 }

To the President of the Confederate States:

In answer to a resolution of the House of Representatives, I have the honor to inclose a list of the civilian prisoners now in custody in this city and in Salisbury, N.C., under military authority. No arrests have been made, at any time, by any specific order or direction of this department. The persons arrested have been taken either by officers of the army commanding in the field or by provost marshals, exercising authority of a similar nature, and the ground of arrest is, or ought to be, founded upon some necessity, or be justified as a proper precaution against an apparent danger. The department has had commissioners to examine these persons, with directions "to discharge those against whom no well-grounded cause of suspicion exists of having violated a law or done an act hostile or injurious to the Confederate States."

The department appointed in November last a commissioner to examine prisoners in the Southwestern Department, embracing a portion of Georgia, Alabama and a portion of Mississippi. This commissioner found some obstructions in the performance of his duties from the provost marshals and some difficulty in obtaining reports from them. He resigned in the latter part of January, without making a report of the prisoners remaining in the department for which he was appointed.

These commissioners have been found useful, and I recommend that the department may be authorized to appoint them for the objects before mentioned, and that they be clothed with the authority of commissioners under the act of the Provincial Congress, No. 273, respecting commissioners appointed by the district courts.

In conclusion, I have to say that under the examinations that have been made a large number of prisoners have been discharged, and none are retained unless there be a cause of suspicion supported by testimony rendering it probable that the discharge of the prisoners

would be prejudicial to the public interest.
>Most respectfully,
>Your obedient servant,
>James A. Seddon,
>Secretary of War.

List of political prisoners at Salisbury, N.C., omitted.

About Suspending the *Habeas Corpus* Writ

Remembering the long and bloody struggle which the friends of liberty have waged in the defense of the privilege of habeas corpus, recognizing it as an inestimable security and protection of the individual against the arbitrary acts of ambitious power, I am, nevertheless, forced to the confession, from my own observation, that occasions may arise when the most devoted defenders of liberty may with propriety, aye, must from necessity, suspend it for the protection of the country.

The fundamental principle and design of all proper government is the well-being and defense of society in its rights and privileges. Occasions may, and often do, arise in time of war or insurrection, when the right to suspend the writ is to be decided by the plain question between a single individual and the whole community. It often happens, further, that while the danger to society and the government is clearly apparent, existing circumstances render a fair and full trial utterly impossible as soon as the public interest may demand.

Such was the case in numerous instances in the Southern Confederacy. Furthermore, arrest and imprisonment in such cases, when they are not attended by the infliction of any punishment beyond what is involved in the restraint of the confinement, are not to be viewed necessarily as a violent deprivation of enjoyment and freedom, but as a prudential deprivation of the opportunity to commit contemplated injury and destruction.

There are cases of reasonable suspicion against an individual when it is impossible to find evidence to justify his imprisonment under the civil law. It would certainly be a suicidal policy for a commander in such cases to wait till his plans are frustrated, his command betrayed and irretrievable losses sustained by some overt act of the supposed traitor or spy before ordering his arrest.

A case of this character occurred in Gen. Whiting's brigade in the latter part of 1861. While posted on the right wing of Johnston's army, one of his regiments encamped near a farm house, where, among others, lived a young man whose countenance betokened a base, designing spirit. I watched him loitering with an air of ill-concealed thoughtfulness about the regiment and suspected from his conduct that he was giving information to the enemy. The suspicion was entertained by the officers, too, but no clue to his guilt could be obtained. On the morning that the long roll beat for the regiment to leave he was seen galloping on the road to the river in great haste – in all probability communicated the movement of the whole force to the enemy and was not arrested till his return.

But while it may sometimes be proper, from the peculiar circumstances, to arrest and confine suspected parties, it cannot be right to postpone the examination of such cases a day longer than is unavoidable. Prompt investigation should decide whether the arrest is "founded upon some necessity," or can be "justified as a proper precaution against an apparent danger." It is believed that the Confederate authorities are censurable for delay in such examination touching the arrest and custody of the civilian prisoners at Salisbury. One case is remembered, as reported by the commissioner when he came [to] Salisbury, of a citizen from western Virginia, who had been in prison for fourteen months, and when his case was examined there was not the shadow of reason for his imprisonment. Mr. Seddon, speaking of the result of the examination in the Southwestern Department, states that "a large number had been discharged." Not recollecting positively, my impression is that a considerable number of those confined at Salisbury, were promptly released when the facts of their arrest were brought to light.

After the departure of Colonel Goodwin for the field, who, like Colonel Gibbs, made the prison guard the nucleus for a fine regiment, Captain McCoy held the office of commandant for some time. He was also quartermaster of the post for a considerable period, and finally held a position on the staff of his relative, General Winder.

The Prison's Better Days

Up to the latter part of 1864, the prison presented few of those horrors which afterwards rendered it so shocking and deplorable. The citizens of Salisbury will long remember how often they have heard the loud songs of the prisoners in those first years, when in the first still hours of the summer night they beguiled the heavy moments in singing those familiar hymns which bring to all hearts the sad, sweet memories of other days and absent friends. Those songs told of sad home thoughts, and there were many, doubtless, who heard them with a kinder sympathy than the singers dreamed.

Coming from the prison they fell on the heart like "a thought of heaven in a field of graves." They called up sacred musings of that Better Land, where peace is never broken and freedom has no foe or fear.

About this period we have the testimony of an escaped prisoner — a newspaper correspondent — that the rations were tolerable both in quality and quantity. The prisoners had the privilege of purchasing a variety of articles from outsiders. The above correspondent says that at one time his mess had seventy-five dozen eggs. During the spring, summer and autumn some of the citizens showed their kindness and humanity by carrying or sending down quantities of provision. The buildings afforded ample shelter, there being, in addition to the large house, six other smaller brick buildings. The old well afforded pure refreshing water, and the oaks shed a cool and grateful shade. An escaped prisoner published a complimentary acknowledgment of the genial courtesy and generosity of Capt. Swift Galloway, who was at that time commanding. They then had for the sick clean hay mattresses, and a frame hospital large enough for forty patients. There was one peculiarly sad feature, however, connected with the prisoners. It was the close confinement of two or three officers as hostages for a like number of Confederate officers whom the Federal government was threatening to execute in retaliation for the death of certain criminals by order of the Confederate authorities. Their lot was of necessity very severe, but was alleviated by the magnanimous treatment of the commandant.

Methods of Escape

There were a few regular prisoners of war at this time in addition to other classes. Twelve officers were confined in the upper story of the large building. They concluded to make a desperate effort to escape. Accordingly they tied their blankets together, hung them out of the window, and a deserter, who was to act as their guide, started down. But the blankets were torn by his weight, he fell to the ground, the sentinels discovered him, and the plan was foiled.

Other attempts were made by means of tunnels, one running from the commissary building to the stockade, but the vigilance of the guards again foiled them. The efforts and plans resorted to in order to affect their escape were often very irregular. The dead were buried outside of the stockade by a detail of prisoners under guard. Upon one of these occasions one of the prisoners, being a ventriloquist, threw his voice into the coffin and so frightened the guards that the escape of the entire detail was easily effected. Another successful plan was known as the "small-pox ruse." The hospital for those afflicted with this dire malady was without the stockade. A number of prisoners, heating some needles red hot, burned small holes in their faces and bodies, and presenting themselves to the surgeon of the post, were ordered to the hospital. Once beyond the stockade, but little time elapsed re they, too, had escaped.

When new deserters were brought to the prison they were generally "mugged" by those already there, and stripped of everything that they had thus far preserved for their comfort. The parties were detected and subjected to severe corporal punishment, but as they continued their rapacious violence, the balance of the prisoners petitioned the authorities to send them to Andersonville. They were sent in compliance, and after reaching Andersonville became so obnoxious that they were arraigned before a court martial of the prisoners, tried for their lives, and six of them were convicted and hung. It might have been one of these who, at Andersonville, murdered his own brother in order to get his property at the North, buried his body in his tent, spread his blanket over it, and for some time slept upon it. A gentleman from Georgia informed me such a case actually occurred.

On March 3rd Capt. J. H. Fuqua was appointed to the duties of inspector, and second in command.

Capt. Galloway was succeeded by Col. John A. Gilmer, who had been so severely wounded in battle that he was unable to perform active service again.

In July the officers of the prison were Col. John A. Gilmer, commandant; Capt. J. H. Fuqua, assistant commandant; Lieut. F. D. Stockton, adjutant.

The prison guard was composed of three companies known as "Freeman's Battalion."

Company A., Capt. C. D. Freeman, 110 men; Company B., Capt. H. P. Allen, 108 men; Company C., Capt. E. D. Snead, 112 men.

The prisoners at that time numbered and were classified as follows: Confederates under sentence of court martial, 310; Yankee deserters, 95; political prisoners, 164.

Inquiries About Political Prisoners

In September Judge Sidney S. Baxter came to Salisbury as commissioner to make inquiry into the cases of the political prisoners. He was eminently qualified from his humane disposition, integrity and talent to discharge the duties of his delicate mission. His voluntary efforts to assist Major Gee, during the next month, in relieving the suffering thousands of the prisoners who were crowded into the stockade, sufficiently attest the fidelity with which he addressed himself to the interest of those unfortunate men whom he was specially commissioned to look after.

Col. Gilmer's health was not sufficient for the duties of the post. I have never heard from any source any complaint against the manner in which he discharged his duties as commandant. In September, 1864, he resigned, and the office of commandant was filled by the appointment of Maj. John H. Gee, of Quincy, Florida. Chief Justice Dupont, of Florida, being in Richmond, soon after this appointment, was told by Gen. Braxton Bragg that there were "a number of hard cases at Salisbury, and Maj. Gee was appointed to that place on account of his prudence and discretion."

About the last of September Maj. Gee received a dispatch from Richmond ordering him to make provisions immediately for a very large number of prisoners. Being a very humane man, he was greatly shocked by the order, for he knew it would be impossible to take care of so many. But bad as the state of affairs at Salisbury, it was vastly worse at Richmond. There the population had become so numerous, and the drain by the army had been and still continued to be so enormous that the question of bare subsistence had become one of alarming interest. One of our Senators stated that, accepting an invitation to eat at the President's table, he found nothing but corn bread and fried bacon for the bill of fare. The condition of many of the citizens was deplorable, and the remnant of the great army of Northern Virginia was compelled to bear hunger while doing four-fold service against a vastly out-numbering army. No wonder then that the protest of Maj. Gee was unheeded.

Determined to do the best he possibly could with the limited means at his command, he addressed himself with earnest endeavor to the task of putting the prison in condition to receive the coming thousands. And that task was indescribably arduous. There were scarcely any axes, shovels, tools, lumber, wells, tents or any other requisite in the place or within his reach. He put a number of men to work with the best implements that could be gotten, to dig more wells. He required them not only to dig by day, but by candle-light at night. The carpenters were also ordered to enlarge the stockade. But before these improvements could be accomplished, immense trains of prisoners began to arrive. By the 5th of October about 5,000 had come. One train, probably the first, brought between one and two hundred officers, of various rank, from brigadier-general down. On the 5th I visited the prison in company with several ladies. The ground was then firm and quite dry, and the place appeared well adapted to the purpose for which it was used. But that was the last time that the place had the appearance of aught but misery and wretchedness. The officers' and privates' respective portions of the grounds were separated by only a line of sentinels — the former occupying the eastern quarter, with the old wooden buildings.

The prisoners were always trying to escape, and not unfrequently they succeeded. Occasionally they would be arrested again by citizens and brought back. Frequently they would reach the mountains, find plenty of friends to supply and direct them, and make their way across the mountains to the Federal lines.

Prison Horrors

When the officers arrived, an attempt was made by robbers to "mug" them under cover of the darkness, as they had done many before; but an alarm was given, and they did not affect their design. These "muggers," as they were termed in the prison parlance, were a regularly organized band of desperate characters, ready to rob the living or the dying, or to commit actual murder to get money, provisions, clothes or other property. Although a number were sent, as before stated, to Georgia, the prison still continued to be infested with them to the last. It will never be known how many of their fellow prisoners they murdered. I think it was not uncommon for marks of violence to be discovered on the bodies of the dead. I saw one laid in the grave who appeared to have been killed by choking. Another, who was very emaciated, had a narrow wound like the incision of a small dagger near the jugular vein. Without this he could not have lived long, and I could divine no reason for his murder but impatience to get possession of clothes or something else which could not be obtained while he was alive.

During the month of October the number of prisoners amounted to 10,321. The regular prisoners of war and the rebel convicts were in perpetual feud, owing to the latter having in September found and seized a Federal flag which one of the prisoners had brought in concealed upon his person. So bitter was this feud that the convicts did not dare to leave their quarters in the large building and venture out in the grounds at night.

There was no great degree of kindness between the Yankee deserters and the convicts. They would gamble together in the upper story of the main building, insult one another, and get into terrible altercations. One of the guards told me that at night walking the parapet, he had heard them fighting, heard the cry of "murder," growing fainter and fainter, and finally heard the gurgling struggles as of men weltering in blood. One night a deserter was thrown from the upper window and taken up dead.

By order of the War Department, Gen. Martin raised about fifteen hundred guards, of whom over a thousand were senior reserves, men between forty-five and fifty, and several hundred junior reserves, who were boys between seventeen and eighteen years of age. Add to these "Freeman's Battalion" and you have all the troops that Major Gee was furnished to control ten thousand regular soldiers. The stockade was simply a plank fence about ten or twelve feet high, so frail in many places that it could be shaken for a long distance by the hand.

It was the opinion of competent judges that a rush by a body of men against it would have broken it down. In some parts the planks at the bottom did not reach the ground, and it required but little effort, as experiment proved, to open a way for egress under them. The senior reserves who comprised the large majority of the guard, were ignorant of discipline, and so old and awkward and unteachable — many of them — that they appeared more like Quixotic burlesques than veritable soldiers. The junior reserves were much more vigilant and efficient, but many of them were exceedingly small and presented quite a grotesque picture as they lugged a huge musket around their beat. But for their diminutive size they would have made excellent sentinels. Freeman's men were all who had enough of the soldier about them to be depended on to discharge all the duties of a guard. Under such circumstances it may well be conceived how anxiously those who were entrusted with the keeping of the prisoners felt their responsibility. From October to the time they left there was no time (except, perhaps, while Col. Hinton with the 68th Regiment was there,) when, acting in concert and with determination, the prisoners could not have overpowered the guard and sacked the town. A knowledge of this fact doubtless caused many a wakeful hour to Major Gee while others were sleeping, and may account for seeming severity in the regulations which were enforced.

When the prisoners came they could not be supplied with a sufficient number of tents, and in consequence they suffered greatly from exposure. In apology for this it must be observed that there was a much larger proportion furnished them then were employed by our own soldiers in the field; and there were really no more that could be procured. As soon as they could be obtained two hundred tents were furnished them — of different kinds — fly, wall and others. Thus did they get what was denied our sons and brothers. After Bradley T. Johnson came he made direct application to Gov. Vance for tents, knowing probably that they could not be obtained from the government, and the Governor, notwithstanding he had taken steps to contribute to the relief of the Salisbury prisoners, was compelled to answer that he had none.

Yankee Ingenuity in Providing Shelter

As they did not have enough houses or tents to shelter them, and the scarcity of tools, teams, lumber and guards for the working parties prevented cabins being constructed, they resorted to "Yankee ingenuity" to provide shelter for themselves. A few crowded under the hospital and other houses, and slept there in bad weather. But the main resort was burrowing in the earth. The whole enclosure was literally honey-combed by these burrows. They were square or round holes dug some three feet deep, with a mud-thatched roof — a hole being punched through to the surface at one end, and a little chimney further built up out of baked earth. Over the entrance there was a little porch or projection that, as long as it withstood the rain itself, kept the water from the main burrow. But for the dampness these places would have been comparatively comfortable — for they shielded the tenant from the winds and rains, and required a very small quantity of wood to make them warm. I have seen a thin matting of shavings which had been whittled with a pocket knife, lying on the floor of some of them. The tenant had either to sit or lie down in them; they were too shallow for him to stand erect. They must have been wretchedly uncomfortable and destructive to health and life in those heavy, incessant rains that fell in January and February, 1865. The hospitals were so crowded, and such numbers died in them, that some preferred to linger and suffer in their sickness in these little cells. Consequently they not unfrequently died there alone, and were not discovered for some days.

[Concluded in Next Sunday's *Observer*]

Sunday, June 4, 1893
Salisbury Prison
A Revolt of the Prisoners
Dr. Mangum's Narrative Ended

Touching Descriptions of the Death Scenes of the Prison and the Horrible Burial in Trenches of Naked and Emaciated Corpses, With only a Branch of a Tree, Perhaps, for a Covering — The Pangs of Hunger — Prisoners Climbed Trees for Acorns and Fished Old Bones Out of the Sewers — The Kindness of the Surgeons — One of Them, Dr. Currie, Laid Down His Life in His Efforts to Heal the Sick and Save the Suffering — A Pathetic Scene When Dr. Mangum Preached to the Prisoners — The Mutiny in the Prison When 16 Captives Were Shot Down Dead and 60 Wounded — Edwin M. Stanton to Blame for the Torture and Death at the Prison in Not Consenting to an Early Exchange of Prisoners — He Was Condemned by Escaped Newspaper Correspondents.

Rev. Dr. A. W. Mangum's story of Salisbury prison in last Sunday's *Observer* closed with a description of the straits the poor prisoners were put to in finding sleeping places at night and shelter from the rains and storms. The prison buildings, it was said, were insufficient to contain the herd of human beings crowded within the stockade, and consequently many of the Northern captives exercised their inventive genius in hollowing out for themselves burrows in the earth. Into these cramped quarters they crowded, and the closing paragraph of the first installment of the article contained a graphic and pathetic description of the frequent instance of some poor creature being found dead in his burrow, life having been extinct, perhaps, for several days. The present installment begins with

An Accident

Maj. Moffatt, who was quartermaster to the prison, with duty to provide shelter, etc., had a chimney begun to the large building. When it had reached the third story, the unsound brick at the bottom gave way, and the whole structure fell. Several were injured and perhaps one killed. The sentinels were ordered to clear the building and keep everybody out — and one, rushing back to get something, paid no attention to the sentinel's warning, was fired at and either killed or wounded. Those who were injured were rescued from the rubbish as soon as possible.

Maj. Moffatt found the greatest difficulty in getting lumber for building purposes, but, having procured some, had ordered the carpenters to put up six buildings, 200 feet in length, 22 feet wide, and 20 feet high. When they were engaged in framing these, Gen. Winder, Commandant of Prisons in this and other States, visited and inspected the prison, pronounced the place unfit for a prison, declared that he would have them moved down in South Carolina, and therefore ordered all improvements to be discontinued. Before the arrangements necessary for their removal were completed, the advance of Sherman became so threatening, and the whole situation so critical that the project was abandoned. It was also contemplated to move the prisoners to a more comfortable site on the Yadkin, but the place in view, on examination, proved ineligible. The Confederacy was in its last struggle — its resources all gone, and therefore, though the condition of the prisoners was wretched and appalling, there was no way to ameliorate it. They were in a miserable plight when they came. Large numbers of them were unable to walk, and had to be carried from the train to the prison. Those who had been confined elsewhere for a long time, were pale, emaciated and dejected. Many of them were very filthy and ragged. Some were without hat or cap or any sign of shoes. The clothing of many was very meagre and of summer texture. A very large proportion had no blankets. Such being their condition it is evident that their sufferings in the cold winter were intolerable. Situated as they were the allowance of wood, according to army regulations, was insufficient. Yet as to fuel most energetic efforts were made to supply them. A train ran regularly on the Western Railroad to transport wood. Fifty or sixty of the prisoners went with it as a detail for loading and unloading. Numbers of wagons were frequently if not constantly employed in hauling wood to them. The wood-yard was immediately on the Central road, near the crossing just west of the stockade. It was carried thence by the prisoners who passed to and fro between a line of sentinels. The wood-master was allowed as large a detail for this purpose as he thought necessary. He stated on oath, that the average quantity furnished the prisoners was 35 or 40 cords per day. According to Gen. Johnston they received more nearly, on an average, the regulation allowance, than the troops who guarded them. Yet exposed as they were, twice or thrice the quantity would not have rendered them comfortable.

When the plan was agreed upon, for the two governments to send supplies to their respective soldiers in prison, Major Gee made out a requisition for ten thousand suits of clothing and sent it to the proper authorities at Richmond. A large supply was received and distributed under the supervision of United States officers, who were paroled for that purpose. In addition to their other ills, they had to bear the pangs of hunger. Just prior to their sudden advent, Major Myers, post commissary, had, in obedience to orders, sent all, or nearly all, his stores to Richmond, Goldsboro and Wilmington. The district from which he was allowed to draw was limited to Surry, Yadkin, Davie, Davidson, Iredell, Rowan, Cabarrus, Stanly, Montgomery and Anson; and, for a time, Stokes and Forsyth counties. From these he had received and shipped to the army vast quantities, and it had now become extremely difficult to procure day by day what was required. With a daily demand of thirteen thousand rations, he often had not a day's supply ahead, and no certain source or means for procuring it. He engaged the mills for miles around to grind for him. He sent out purchasing and impressing agents with rigid instructions. He wrote to various points for assistance. He went or sent daily to the depot and train to impress the passing supplies. He, on one occasion, seized some stores that were on the train en route to Lee's army. He joined Major Gee in his protest about more prisoners coming. He begged, entreated, warned, threatened the people to extort provisions from them. I have seen him in the heavy rain, dashing hither and thither, striving to meet the requisitions that were made upon him. When the condition of the people was such that he could neither buy nor impress, he would borrow from them. At first the ration was 1 1/8 w. flour, 1 lb. beef or 1-3 w. bacon (or in lieu of meat when it could not be had 1 w. potatoes or 1 ½ gills sorghum — and to every hundred men 10 lbs. rice and 3 qts. Salt. As the scarcity grew more pressing the flour was reduced one pound or meal was taken. That was in December. Sometimes several days would elapse without Maj. Myers being able to procure any meat. The same rations were issued to the guard as to the prisoners. Indeed, if preference was shown, it was in favor of the prisoners. When Col. Folk had returned from his imprisonment and visited the Salisbury prison, he pronounced the rations more in quantity than he had ever received in a Northern prison. In addition the prisoners were sometimes the recipients of humane offerings by the citizens, and had the liberty, when outside, to purchase, at least occasionally, from the numerous hucksters that hung around the garrison.

Climbing Oaks for Acorns

Yet after all this, they suffered intensely from hunger. They would climb the oaks for acorns and fish from the filthy sewers the crusts and the bones. The sick especially suffered, as what they got was often so coarse that they could not eat it.

Although such efforts were made to provide water, the supply was insufficient for drinking, cooking and washing. Wells were dug until they drained one another. The prisoners were allowed, under guard, to cross the bridge and get water from the wells in town. Those that were near the prison were often kept low and muddy by their constant drawing. They were allowed to go in squads, as numerous as could be guarded with the small number of the garrison, to the creek which ran within a few hundred yards of the place. From there they brought water in barrels. They were going and returning all through the day. Strenuous efforts were made to have the creek turned to run through the grounds, but Major Turner, on examination, pronounced it impracticable with the means at hand. One of the guard was detailed to try to obtain a pump of sufficient capacity for the purpose, but he could not find one.

The hospital accommodations were not such as were desired by the prison officials, and were greatly inadequate to the necessities of so large a number of men so unfavorably situated. The buildings were too small, there was a limited supply of bunks and covering and even straw, and withal a distressing scarcity of medicines. Time after time were requisitions made for these articles upon the proper officials, but with very little success. The United States had made medicines contraband of war — a remarkable innovation on the rules of civilized warfare — and the meagre and irregular medical stores that ran the blockade were their sole dependence (outside of captures by the army) for the supply of the scores of thousands of the sick and wounded who were weltering in homes and hospitals all over the bleeding, panting South. The humane surgeons of the prison had but little margin for the exercise of their professional skill. Their dispensary was painfully scant and ill-furnished. As they looked upon the empty bottles and bare shelves, they must have mused often and painfully of the vast repositories of those articles which would save those men's lives, hoarded in the warehouses of their kinsmen and fellow-citizens at the North, and denied by the government which they had imperiled all to defend. When demands were made upon Capt. Goodman for straw and lumber for bunks, he urged the improbability of obtaining either. The hospital on the second floor of the large building was fitted with good bunks, and two or three of the smaller ones had bunks also. One of them was better supplied than the hospital for the guard.

Gen. Bradley T. Johnston, who by appointment took command of the post on the 24th of December,

'64, was a true gentleman with a generous, sympathetic heart, and joined his strenuous exertions to those of other officials to alleviate the sufferings of the prisoners. He complained heavily of the quartermaster to Gen. Gardner for his inefficiency and deplored the necessity of the sick having sometimes to lie on the bare floor. If all the efforts made by Drs. Currie and Wilson, Maj. Gee and Gen. Johnston to have the hospitals furnished were known, it would speak loudly in their honor and silence the maledictions of those who say that the prisoners suffered from inhumanity instead of necessity. Capt. Goodman may or may not have done the best he could. His good teams were taken away from him and broken-down stock put in their places. The roads were almost impassable. Straw was scarce. The saw mills were not competent to the constant demands upon them. His wagons had to be used for various indispensable purposes. It may safely be affirmed that a far more efficient man would not have been able to meet the overwhelming requisitions made upon him in the general dilapidation and scarcity.

A Surgeon Gave His Life for the Prisoners

The surgeons were faithful and humane, by the admission of the prisoners themselves. Dr. Richard O. Currie, from Knoxville, established a most enviable reputation by his self-sacrificing efforts, as chief surgeon, to minister to the poor sufferers. They seemed to burden his heart continually. He visited them with the spirit of his Savior. A good physician, he ministered to them in sickness — an earnest preacher of the Gospel, he strove to instruct them in the way of life. So incessant and exhausting were his cares and labors for them that, at the close of a day of overpowering toil, he was violently attacked with brain fever, and in a few days passed from his noble toils to the Land of Rest — dying a martyr to the Federal prisoners.

His successor, Dr. Wilson, was also a kind-hearted, faithful, Christian surgeon. After the main body of the prisoners had left, I received an invitation from him to hold divine service for the sick in the basement of the large building. At his request I had before held services in the main grounds. In the hospital were a considerable number of sick, some on bunks and some on the floor. Those on the floor were not REQUIRED but PERMITTED to lie there, as they preferred it. The floor was clean, and, considering the means at his disposal, the apartment was in good condition. He accompanied me and remained to the close of the services. At his request I visited a dying prisoner who had been removed to a good bunk in the guard hospital. After conversing with him freely, when in the act of leaving, I could not but be impressed with the affecting and trustful attachment he evinced for Dr. Wilson, as he begged me to find him and send him to him. I did so, and the doctor went promptly.

The mead of professional fidelity is due to all his assistant surgeons.

But there was terrible mortality in the prison. From the 1st of October, 1864, to the 17th of February, 1865, there were 3,419 deaths among the prisoners. The number of daily deaths varied from eighteen to forty. On one day about sixty-five died. In its worst days the condition of the prison was shocking — the appearance and sufferings of the prisoners harrowing in the extreme. The red clay soil held the water, and under the tramp of thousands became one scene of mud. In December a number of prisoners were detailed to police the enclosure, but so boggy was the whole surface that they could do but little. Ditching would not drain the ground sufficiently.

The prisoners were the very personification of forlorn wretchedness. They seemed to grow more and more dejected, and an ennui congealed the very springs of life. Doomed to inevitable idleness and inactivity, with no sight but such as aggravated the gloom and horror of their shrouded hearts, with hope deferred from week to week, from month to month, many of them sank under the sheer burden of despair, and with a stolid silence and indifference to time or eternity, finished their mortal sorrows in death.

Preaching to the Prisoners

The insensate stupidity of the dying was remarkable. Major Gee informed me in February that he had made careful inquiry, and that of more than three thousand who had died not one had uttered a syllable of concern about the future destiny of his soul. Few religious advantages were afforded them. Dr. Currie preached in the hospitals. On repeated applications to him he discouraged me as to preaching to the masses of the prisoners, stating that they were generally foreigners and Catholics, and were not at all likely to give me a kindly reception. Rev. Dr. Rumple, I think, held service in the hospital for them. In February I was invited by Dr. Wilson to preach to them, he telling me that it had all the time been Major Gee's pleasure for them to have preaching, and that they would certainly appreciate it. Entering the yard on the next afternoon, it being a beautiful Sabbath, I found a Baptist minister near the old well preaching to a large congregation of them; but as there were thousands scattered over the grounds who were not attending, I went to a large oak in the eastern centre and began to sing. A number had followed me and the throng increased for some time. It was to me an interesting occasion. They were very respectful, earnest and solemn. I used the last Testament I had, and telling them during the discourse that I intended presenting it to one of them, I was touched by their eagerness to get it, quite a number pressing up with expectant looks. When I concluded they crowded thickly around me, and a number grasped my hand in Christian fervor.

It was probably Dr. Currie who made an effort for a prison library, and I wrote to the Tract Society at Richmond to get reading for them. Rev. Mr. Bennett was gone to Europe to made arrangements to get some Bibles and Testaments, which were also virtually contraband of war according to the regulation and practice of the United States.

I was answered by Rev. Mr. Moorman. He deplored his inability to supply me from the exhaustion of his supply. He spoke with Christian sympathy of my purpose. Hence few were the Christian privileges of the miserable prisoners. But I have seen the light of heaven in the eye of the suffering captive, and heard from his lips the glorious eloquence of salvation. From the tongue of another I have listened to the rich avowals of Christian hope and confidence, and heard the failing, almost inaudible voice mutter, "Come unto me all yet that labor and are heavy laden, and I will give you rest.' These are precious words." And doubtless amid the gloom and horror of that old prison, there was many an upward glance of the heart — many a struggle and triumph of faith — many a thrill of redeeming love and heavenly hope, which all unknown to friend or foe, were recognized by Him whose nature is love, and who is "mighty to save."

There was a small brick building near the centre of the prison, which was used as a receptacle for the dead until they were carried to the burial ground. They were hauled thence, without coffins, to the old field west of the prison. A detail, first of convicts and afterwards of prisoners of war, was kept day by day, constantly digging the long pits in which they were interred. These pits were four feet deep, a little over six feet wide, and were extended, parallel, about sixty yards. The bodies were laid in them without covering — there was not material to cover the living, much less the dead. They were laid side by side, as closely as they would lie, and when the number was too large for the space that was dug, one would be placed on top between every two. They generally had very little clothing on, as the living were permitted to take their garments. Seldom does it fall to the lot of man to behold a more sickening and heart-rending spectacle than they presented. It was a lesson on the vanity of this life more impressive and eloquent than tongue or pen can describe. It was a picture of the hellish curse of war, in one of its most horrible and hideous aspects. I begged the workmen at least to get some brushes to lay over their faces. Sadly have I mused, as I stood and gazed upon their attenuated forms, as they seemed the very romance of the horrible in shroudless, coffinless grave. Those long, bony hands, were once the dimpled pride of a devoted mother, and on that cold, blanched brow tender love had often pressed the kiss of a mother's lips. Perhaps while I gazed on their hapless fate, a fond wife and prattling children were watching for the mail that they might receive the longed for tidings from him who was best beloved. But I turn from the theme, as I always turned from those harrowing, chilling burials, with a heart full of sadness, and shuddering over the unwritten terrors and calamities of war.

From the congregated evils of imprisonment the prisoners were always anxiously seeking to escape. Gladly did they accept any opportunity to get out, however laborious the duties for which they were detailed. Numbers of them were on parole or detail for various duties. Some were clerks, some in the workshops, some in the shoe factories, some digging graves, some hauling wood on the train, etc., etc.

A Col. Tucker came there for the purpose of getting recruits from their number for the Confederate army. Only foreigners were allowed to enlist. Nearly eighteen hundred took the oath administered by a Catholic priest. Some may have taken this step in good faith, as it is known they were often recruited by foul means in the United States, but the greater number chose it as the only means of escape from their terrible den. They were called "galvanized Yankees," and though most of them made scarcely a show of fighting when the test came, a few stood their ground and fought with true courage.

Escapes From the Prison

Of the whole number in the prison, five or six hundred escaped during the five months from October to March. They sometimes succeeded in deceiving the sentinels and passing quietly out at the gate. One morning a ladder was found against the stockade on the inside. How many had scaled it is not known.

They were constantly engaged in tunneling. At one time they were engaged on sixteen tunnels in different parts of the enclosure. Sometimes whey would complete them and a number escape. But to prevent this a second line of sentinels was placed about thirty feet from the stockade. There were also spies among them who were bribed by the prison officials to detect and betray them.

Before the officers were removed and when there was only a line of sentinels between the officers and privates, a sentinel saw a paper thrown across by an officer, and on examining it, found that it contained directions for an outbreak to be made at a certain signal that night. I have heard that the purpose was to overpower the guard and sack or burn the town. The plot was conceived by General Hays and others. It caused the officers to be removed to Danville immediately. It is almost impossible to conceive what the fate of the unsuspecting citizens would have been that night if the fearful plan had been consummated.

On the 20th of October, about 2 o'clock in the afternoon, as the relief for the inside guard entered the prison, they were rushed upon and disarmed by the prisoners, and two or three of them were killed. One was bayonetted, another shot, and both staggered out to the gate, fell and expired. About eight men were wounded. One sentinel on the parapet was also shot and killed, the ball passing first through the plank. As the prisoners made the rush they raised a tremendous yell. Then came their rapid fire upon the guard. They also threw brickbats and baked earth-balls, whatever they could obtain, at the sentinels. The latter stood to their posts, dodging and firing. In a moment the cannon at one of the angles fired, but being loaded with solid shot it did no execution.

There were soon two more discharges with grape and canister which did terrible execution. The musketry firing by the sentinels also became rapid. A large body of prisoners had congregated in a threatening attitude before the main entrance. As soon as they saw they could not succeed they threw up their hands and cried: "We give up! We are done!" They ran scampering all over the grounds, seeking for shelter, running into their burrows and tents, falling in the ditches and on the ground. The citizens, apprehending the cause of the yells and firing, armed themselves as soon as possible and young and old came in haste to the prison. Col. Hinton's regiment, which was on the train at the depot and about to leave, formed at the sound of the cannon, double-quicked to the stockade and mounted the parapet. But these and the citizens came too late. It is well they were no nearer, no sooner there, for many more would certainly have been killed. The officers of the prison stopped the firing as soon as they possibly could.

About 16 of the prisoners were killed and 60 wounded. It was difficult to restrain the excited people and soldiers, particularly some of Freeman's men whose comrades had been slain. When the prisoners attacked the guard a Yankee deserter knocked one prisoner down with a brickbat, and wrenching a musket from another pinioned him with the bayonet. He then ran to his quarters.

Some of the guard, in running out, made a stand at the gate with some picks and shovels lying there and kept the prisoners back.

The whole affair lasted but about ten minutes. The reason of their signal failure was their want of concert and organization.

An Exchange of Prisoners

About the middle of February, Maj. Gee received intelligence that the articles of exchange had been agreed on. The perpetual dream and longing of those who survived was about to be realized at last. Oh how they had wished and prayed for it! Wading in the mire, pinched by hunger, chilled with cold, covered with vermin, broken in spirit, the thought of home was as sweet as the vision of happiness, and their most eager inquiry of all visitors was, "Is there any prospect for exchange?" At last their sad hearts were to be gladdened. Maj. Gee, knowing how it would excite and transport them, charged the officer who was to inform them to warn them to make no demonstrations lest the guard might fire upon them. His message was, "Tell them they have something good to sleep over tonight."

About the 20th, all who were well enough, were removed. The sick were carried on the trains. The hospitals were emptied of all who could travel. It was a pitiable spectacle to see the haggard, staggering patients marching to the train. Some faltered along alone; some walked in couples, supporting one another; now and then three would come together, the one in the middle dragged along by the other two; and occasionally several would bear a blanket on which was stretched a friend unable to walk or stand. Deeply was every heart stirred which was not dead to sympathy, as the throng gazed on the heartrending pageant. God forbid I should ever be called to witness the like again! At the train they received refreshments from the hands of several citizens. About 2,800 started to march to Greensboro. A great many who started were unable to make the march. Besides the stragglers, two hundred were left at Lexington and five hundred the next day, were abandoned on the road. About one thousand failed on the way.

I have failed to mention that three or four hundred negroes were brought to the prison, and were treated precisely as the other prisoners of war.

After this general delivery about 500 were confined, some of them from Sherman's army, and were hurried to Charlotte just in time to escape Stoneman's raiders in April. The day that Stoneman captured Salisbury his prisoners were penned in the very same stockade which had so long enclosed the hordes of Federal captives. All the buildings and the stockade were burned by Stoneman's orders on the night of the 12th of April. A number of his men had been imprisoned there, and doubtless some of them were in the detail to which was assigned the avenging torch.

Having written thus frankly of the dark history of this great reservoir of misery and death, I now ask, "Who is to blame?" And I answer in the very words of two escaped prisoners, newspaper correspondents, who published their prison experience after their return to the North.

Escaped Prisoners Blamed Edwin M. Stanton

Mr. Richardson says: "The government held a large excess of prisoners and the rebels were anxious to exchange man for man, but our authorities acted upon the cold-blooded theory of Edwin M. Stanton, Secretary of War, that we could not afford to give well-fed, rugged men for invalids and skeletons — that returned prisoners were infinitely more valuable to the rebels than to us, because their soldiers were inexorably kept in the army, while many of ours, whose term of service had expired, would not reenlist."

Mr. Brown writes: "As soon as Mr. Richardson and myself reached our lines we determined to visit Washington, even before returning to New York, to see what could be done for the poor prisoners we had left behind, and determine what obstacles there had been in the way of an exchange. We were entirely free. We owed nothing to the rebels or to the government for our release. We had obtained our own liberty, and were very glad of it, for we believed our captives had been so unfairly, not to say inhumanely, treated at Washington that we were unwilling to be indebted to the authorities of that city for our emancipation. We went to Washington, deferring everything else to move in the matter of prisoners, and did what we thought most effective for the end we had in view. During our sojourn there we made it our special business to inquire into the causes of the detention of Union prisoners in the South, although it was known that they were being deliberately starved and frozen by the rebels. We particularly endeavored to learn who was responsible for the murder — for it was nothing else — of thousands of our brave soldiers; and we did learn. There was but one answer to all our questions, and that was, Edwin M. Stanton, Secretary of War. Although he knew the exact condition of affairs in the rebel prisons, he always insisted that we could not afford to exchange captives with the South; that it was not policy. Perhaps it was not; but it was humanity, and possibly that is almost as good as policy in other eyes than Mr. Stanton's. After our departure from Washington, such a storm was raised about the Secretary's ears — such a tremendous outside feeling was created — that he was compelled to make an exchange.

"The greater part of the Northern prisoners have now been released, I believe, but there was no more reason why they should have been paroled or exchanged since February than there was ten or twelve months ago. No complications, no obstacles had been removed in the meantime. Our prisoners might just as well have been released a year since as a month since, and if they had been, thousands of lives would have been saved to the republic, not to speak of those near and dear ones who were materially and spiritually dependent upon them.

"Dreadful responsibility for some one; and that some one, so far as I can learn, is the Secretary of War. I hope I may be in error, but cannot believe I am. If I am right, heaven forgive him! for the people will not. The ghosts of the thousands needlessly sacrificed heroes will haunt him to his grave."

As these extracts are against the officers of their own government, one, if not both, written when the storm had lulled and the mind was capable of dispassionate reflection and judgment, we, of course, must accept them as true. They agree with and corroborate the opinion of all well-informed persons at the South — thus making it the verdict of the jury of the millions North and South, that Edwin M. Stanton, and not the authorities of the Confederacy, is guilty of the deliberate destruction of thousands of Federal and Confederate captives whom he would not permit to be exchanged.

Why, then, all this unrelenting bitterness — this bloodthirsty, inexorable vengefulness towards the South? Impartial history will show that in the article of prisons, she was "more sinned against than sinning." It is known by all who choose to know the truth, that stern necessity and insupportable national misfortunes occasioned the sufferings of Federal captives in Southern prisons. The South, both citizens and government, clamored for exchange — the North refused it.

But where is the apology for the barbarities and murders of Northern prisons? Is it found in the *lex talionis*? Where is the authority that justifies retaliation against inevitable necessity?

SALISBURY, N. C., February 17, 1865.
General S. COOPER,
Adjutant and Inspector General C. S. Army:

GENERAL:

I have the honor to acknowledge the receipt at Charlotte on the 11th instant of letter of instructions of February 10, from Colonel R. H. Chilton, inclosing a communication from His Excellency the Governor of North Carolina to the Honorable Secretary of War, in regard to the suffering condition of the Federal prisoners at this post, and directing me to make an immediate inspection of the prison and full report of the subject. I have the honor to state that acting under my previous general instructions of December 5, 1864, and January 19, 1865. I included the condition of the military prison and treatment of the prisoners of war there confined in the general inspection of the post, in which I was engaged from the 1st to the 10th of February, and the results of my observations would have been immediately forwarded to the Department but for the fact that the post commander, Brigadier General Bradley T. Johnson, happened to be absent from the post during the whole time of my inspection, and I deemed it not less in accordance with the spirit of my instructions than the dictates of military propriety to withhold my report until I should have an opportunity of conferring with him upon the subject and of ascertaining how far it might be in his power to remedy the evils found to exist. Pending his return I was engaged in an inspection of the post of Charlotte, but immediately upon the receipt of Colonel Chilton's letter returned to this place, and on the 16th instant made a second inspection of the prison in company with General Johnson. The results of my two visits in company with General Johnson. The results of my two visits of inspection are respectfully submitted as follows:

I made three visits of inspection to the prison-January 31, in company with Major Mason Morfit, prison quartermaster; February 1, in company with Major J. H. Gee, prison commandant, and the medical officer of the prison, and again, as already stated, on the 16th of February, with General B. T. Johnson. On the two occasions first named the weather was particularly pleasant and I saw the prison under the most favorable circumstances. On the 16th of February, immediately after a fall of snow and sleet, I saw it again, probably in its worst aspect. In my report I have endeavored carefully to distinguish between those causes of suffering which are unavoidable, and for the existence of which, therefore, the Government and its officers cannot be held responsible, and such abuses as, in my opinion, are justly chargeable to the neglect or inefficiency of the prison management.

I. Location and plan of the prison.-The location of the prison I regard as an unfortunate one, though I presume this with the Government at the time was a matter not of choice but of necessity. That it was already as a prison for civilians and military convicts should have been an argument against its selection, not in its favor, unless it had been at the same time determined to remove the former classes of prisoners. The general plan of the prison may be seen from the diagram accompanying this report. The area inclosed and constituting the main prison yard is about eleven acres. I do not think, especially with the present number of prisoners (5,476 of all classes), that there can be any reasonable ground of complaint on the score of want of room. Water is obtained from nine wells within the inclosure and from the creek, one mile and a half distant, to which the prisoners are allowed to go, a certain number at a time, under guard, with buckets and barrels. The supply obtained from all these sources, however, is not more than sufficient for cooking and drinking purposes. The want of a running stream within the prison inclosure, for the purposes of washing and general sewerage, is therefore a serious objection. The proximity of the prison to the railroad affords every necessary facility for obtaining an adequate supply of fuel, which can be deposited in any quantity needed within less than 100 yards of the prison, and unloaded and transported by the labor of the prisoners themselves. A memorandum statement of Major Morfit, prison quartermaster, accompanying this report, shows the amount of fuel received, issued, and due the prisoners from January 1 to February 15, 1865. That they have not received the full amount due them during a season of more than ordinary inclemency I think is chargeable more probably to want of energy on the part of the post quartermaster, Captain J. M. Goodman, than to any other cause. Both Major Gee and Major Morfit profess to consider the actual supply sufficient, but in this I think they are mistaken. The fact cited by Major Gee that the prison sutler buys all his fuel from the prisoners proves nothing, no more than their willingness to part with their newly received supplies of clothing, a practice to check which General Johnson has been obliged to publish a stringent order forbidding citizens or soldiers from purchasing, proves that they are not in want of clothes.

The most serious objection to this choice of a site for a prison is, however, the character of the soil, which is a stiff, tenacious red clay, difficult of drainage and which remains wet for a long time, and after a rain or snow becomes a perfect bog. The system of drainage contemplates the double object of carrying off the surface water and cleansing the sinks, but cannot be said to be particularly successful in either point of view. In warm weather or in a season of drought the sinks would not fail to prove a source of great annoyance, and possibly of pestilence, not only in the prison, but in the town of Salisbury.

II. The prison commissariat.-Among the papers accompanying this report will be found a statement of the number of rations issued from February 1 to February 15, 1865, showing the component parts of the ration and the quantity of each. Compared in quantity and kind with the rations issued to our own troops in the field, it will be seen that on this score the prisoners have no cause to complain. The rations are cooked before they are issued, and pains have been taken by General Johnson to see that no frauds are committed in this department to the injury of the prisoners. Bread and meat (or sorghum in lieu of meat) are issued every morning, rice or pea soup in the afternoon. The bread which I inspected in the bakery was of average quality and of the average weight of five pounds to the double loaf. A half loaf, therefore, the daily allowance of each prisoner, will average twenty ounces of bread, the equivalent of sixteen ounces of flour.

III. Clothing.-More than from any other cause the prisoners have suffered this winter from the want of sufficient and suitable clothing, being generally destitute of blankets and having only such clothes as they wore when captured, which, in the case of many of them, was during warm weather. Recently 3,000 blankets and 1,000 pair of pants have been received from the United States and are now being distributed under the supervision of three Federal officers sent here from Danville for the purpose. Additional supplies are expected, and it is probable that one principal cause of suffering will therefore soon be removed, one for which, however, the Confederate Government is under no circumstances chargeable, but which is ascribable solely to the neglect of their own Government. As already stated, General Johnson has taken every necessary step to prevent speculation upon the necessities of the prisoners by prohibiting all purchases from them of articles of clothing by soldiers or citizens.

IV. Prison quarters.-Three hundred tents and flies of mixed sizes and patterns were issued for the use of the prisoners of war in October by Major Morfit, prison quartermaster, and constitute the only shelter provided during the winter for a number of prisoners, amounting on the 7th of November to 8,740, and the 15th of February to 5,070. Major Morfit showed me the frame of a large barrack, of which he told me he had contemplated erecting five for the accommodation of the prisoners, but was stopped by an order two months ago from the Commissary-General of Prisoners, intimating the possibility of a speedy removal of the prisoners, and ordering all work of the kind to be suspended. The prisoners were not removed, and in my judgment if General Winder's order had never been issued Major Morfit's plan would have been found, in its conception, to involve great and unnecessary expense to the Government, probably not less than $75,000 or $100,000, and in its execution would probably have consumed the entire winter, and therefore have resulted in little practical benefit to the prisoners. A better plan would have been, failing to obtain a sufficient supply of tents, to have constructed cabins of pine logs and shingles, for which the material was at hand in abundance, and labor could have been furnished by the troops, or, if necessary, by details of the prisoners themselves, working under guard. In this way the garrison who guard the prisoners have been made comfortable; so might have been the prisoners. I cannot consider it, therefore, a matter of choice on their own part, that at the time of my inspection I found one-third of the latter burrowing like animals in holes under ground or under the buildings in the inclosure.

V. Prison hospitals.-One of the most painful features connected with the prison is the absence of adequate provision or accommodation for the sick. There is no separate hospital inclosure, but with a few exceptions, as will be seen from the diagram, all the buildings in the prison yard are used as hospitals. The number sick in hospital February 15 was 546. There was an entire absence of hospital comforts-bedding, necessary utensils, etc. The reason assigned on the occasion of my first visit (February 1) was, that it was useless to supply these articles as no guard was kept inside of the prison yard and they would be inevitably stolen. Surg. John Wilson, Jr., the medical officer at present in charge, is endeavoring to supply these deficiencies, and in the short interval of two weeks between my first and second visits had succeeded in effecting several improvements. Still much remains to be done. There are bunks for not more than one-half of the sick, the rest lie upon the floor or ground, with nothing under them but a little straw, which on February 16 had not been changed for four weeks. For a period of nearly one month in December and January the hospitals, I was told, were without straw. For this there is no excuse. I am satisfied that straw could have been obtained in abundance at any time, the county (Rowan) being one of the largest wheat-growing counties in the State, and I am assured by Captain Crockford, inspector of field transportation in this department, that the field transportation at this post has been in excess heretofore of the requirements of the post; that in January, when no straw was furnished, he found thirty animals standing idle in Captain Goodman's stable, and consequently ordered them to be turned over. The excessive rate of mortality among the prisoners, as shown by the prison returns herewith forwarded, merits attention. Out of 10,321 prisoners of war received since October 5, 1864, according to the surgeon's report, 2,918 have died. According to the burial report, since the 21st of October 1864, a less period by sixteen days, 3,479 have been buried. The discrepancy is explained by the fact than in addition to the deaths in hospital, six or eight die daily in the quarters without the knowledge of the surgeons, and of course without receiving attention from them. This discrepancy, which in December amounted to 223, and in January to 192, in the first two weeks of February had diminished to 21. The actual number of deaths, however, outside of hospital during that period would show probably little falling off, if any, from the number in previous months. Pneumonia and diseases of the bowels are the prevalent diseases. The prisoners appear to die, however, more from exposure and exhaustion than from actual disease.

VI. Prison discipline.-Inside of the prison there appears to be no proper system of discipline or police. The prisoners are divided into the divisions, each division into as many squads, the divisions in charge of a sergeant-major of their own number, the squads under a sergeant. Two roll-calls are nominally observed, the one in the morning being usually neglected. In the afternoon the prisoners are mustered by squads and counted by the prison clerk and his assistants. No details are made for the purpose of policing the grounds, except one of a sergeant and twelve men, who report to the surgeon. All sorts of filth are allowed to be deposited and to remain anywhere and every-where around the quarters, unsightly to the eye and generating offensive odors and in time, doubtless, disease. Since the outbreak of November 25, no guard is kept inside the inclosure, except at the gates. Robberies and murders even are said to be of not unfrequent occurrence among the prisoners, usually charged to an association of the worst characters among them, known as "Muggers." But a few days before my first visit a negro prisoner in one of the hospital wards was murdered by one of these ruffians, and such is the state of terrorism inspired that none of the patients or attendants in the ward who saw the deed would lodge information against the murderer, who was at last only discovered and arrested through the agency of a detective.

    The use of detective and a counter association among the prisoners are the only dependence of the commandant for enforcing any kind of order, discipline, or police in the prison. The excuse given by Major Gee for not having the prison grounds properly policed was the want of tools and the danger of trusting picks, etc., in the hands of the prisoners. The excuse cannot be considered sufficient; wooden scrapers and hickory brooms, with wheelbarrows or boxes with rope handles, all of which can readily be furnished by the prison quarter, would answer every purpose. I subsequently brought the matter to the attention of General Johnson, who promised to issue the necessary orders upon the subject and see that they are enforced. Major Gee, the prison commandant, as an officer, is deficient in administrative ability, but in point of vigilance, fidelity, and in everything that concerns the security of the prison and the safe keeping of the prisoners, leaves nothing to be desired. As respects the general question of the condition of the prisoners I am of the opinion that so far as their sufferings have resulted from causes within the control of the Government or its officers they are chargeable (1) to the unfortunate location of the prison, which is wholly unsuitable for the purpose; (2) to the want of administrative capacity, proper energy and effort on the part of the officers of the Quartermaster's Department charged with the duty of supplying the prison.

To attempt an exact apportionment of the blame in this respect between Major Mason Morfit, the prison quartermaster, and Captain James M. Goodman, the post quartermaster, would probably be irrelevant to the purpose of the present report. Having had occasion in a general inspection of the post of Salisbury to examine the affairs of both of these officers, I cannot say that I consider either of them as efficient in his present position.

I have the honor to be, general, very respectfully, your obedient servant,

T. W. HALL,
Assistant Adjutant and Inspector General.

Note: Misspellings or grammar in this letter have not been changed.

Adolphus W. Mangum

In 1861 as a 27 year old, Adolphus W. Mangum enlisted in the 6th North Carolina Infantry where he served as chaplain of his regiment. Prior to the war he had obtained a Doctor of Divinity degree and had been serving as a Methodist minister in Salisbury.

Mangum left the army in October 1861 due to illness and returned to Salisbury. He began serving as chaplain of the Salisbury Prison, tending to Federal prisoners while keeping records and diaries. In Louis Brown's 1992 book *The Salisbury Prison*, Brown quoted much information recorded by Mangum.

In 1875 Mangum joined the faculty of the University of North Carolina. A debilitating stroke in 1889 forced him to retire from teaching.

On May 12, 1890, he passed away and is buried in the old Chapel Hill Cemetery in Orange County.

www.ingramcontent.com/pod-product-compliance
Lightning Source LLC
Chambersburg PA
CBHW052105110526
44591CB00013B/2360